before & after

ONE MOTHER'S STORY OF
LOVE, LOSS, AND HEALING

MICHELE TRUMPOUR

 FriesenPress

Suite 300 - 990 Fort St
Victoria, BC, V8V 3K2
Canada

www.friesenpress.com

ISBN
978-1-5255-9275-1 (Hardcover)
978-1-5255-9274-4 (Paperback)
978-1-5255-9276-8 (eBook)

1. FAMILY & RELATIONSHIPS, DEATH, GRIEF, BEREAVEMENT

Distributed to the trade by The Ingram Book Company

INTRODUCTION

Writing a book was never on my bucket list. I'm not a writer. I'm a mom with a story.

After my son Tyler died, I was overwhelmed with emotions that I could not comprehend. Journaling became my way of processing these feelings and helped me with healing. Then one day, a voice inside me told me to write a book. I tried to ignore it. I argued with that voice, trying to convince it otherwise. Writing a book and sharing my story scared the wits out of me. After five years, that voice still hadn't left me. So, I wrote a book.

This is not a perfectly written book. But then, this is not a perfect story. By sharing my journey, others have shared theirs, and I've learned that perhaps no one has a perfect story. My intention is to make sharing our imperfect worlds a little more acceptable. There is great solace in connection and telling our stories.

To say that it was difficult to write about my grief is a vast understatement. I would stare at the page, struggling to find words that would accurately reflect the magnitude of my pain. Even harder than writing about my grief was sharing the story of Tyler's addiction. I feared that some people might view the loss of his life as less significant—a loss that should have been easier to accept. But then something shifted and I felt *compelled* to tell my story. By honoring my imperfect journey, I've found immense emotional freedom, with lightness and calm. I hope that others will be inspired to do the same.

My son's addiction did not lessen my grief. My son's addiction did not take away from the person that he was—a young man who loved talking to people, all people from all walks of life . . . who loved to laugh . . . who had a sensitive heart . . . who loved the outdoors . . . who was athletic, handsome, and smart. Yes, it was harder to see this person at the height of his addiction, but a mother never loses the essence of her child. Had he lived, I might have lost him anyways. I may have grieved, not for the loss of his life, but for the loss of him. Both ways are inconceivable to a parent.

So, I write this book for all those who are struggling silently. I write this book for all the moms trying too hard to be perfect moms. I write this book for anyone grieving and feeling like no one can possibly understand.

Most of all, I write this book for Tyler. I love you now and always, my beautiful boy.

1

APRIL 24TH

FRIDAY, APRIL 24, 2015 – This is the day my life was forever changed. This is the day my son, Tyler, died. Cause of death: fentanyl overdose. He had just turned 25.

I have relived the agony of that day a million times over. It was a Friday—another ordinary day. I headed off to work at my usual 7:45 a.m. departure. With a five-minute commute, I could still arrive a few minutes early—one of the great perks of living in a small city. This was the same drive, to the same office, that I had made for the past 12 years. That year, I would celebrate 20 years with the same company. We had moved to Camrose, Alberta, in 2002 when I was given the opportunity to step into a managerial role. It was a job with challenges, but I felt grateful to work for a great company, doing something I enjoyed. Even so, I was always excited about Fridays, knowing the weekend was around the corner. That weekend was even more exciting because I would be running a 10-kilometre race. I enjoyed the atmosphere of these events—the excitement, the energy. I did not fit the mould of a natural "runner," and I'm not even sure that I liked running.

It was the sense of accomplishment when the run was over that fuelled my passion. I had set a lofty goal to run a marathon later that summer, and this run would be a good kickoff to my training plan. So, as I worked through my list of tasks, I was feeling especially good that day. Only a couple more hours until 5:00 p.m. Little did I know that this was the last time anything would feel "normal" again for a very long time.

A little after 3:00 p.m., my manager, Alan, came to my office. Without any preamble, he simply asked, "Can you come to Grant's office for a minute?" Nothing struck me as unusual. Grant was on our management team and together we regularly discussed new issues or sought each other's opinions. Alan seemed solemn, so I was prepared for something a bit more serious. But nothing could have possibly prepared me. I followed him down the hallway. As we approached Grant's office, I could see several silhouettes of people through the frosted glass door. This was the first moment that I sensed something was "off." Alan opened the door for me but did not follow me. Grant left the room quickly before I could see his face. I know now that he did not want me to see his tears.

I was alone with two police officers and two strangers. I knew instantly that they were volunteers from Victim Services. My body started to shake uncontrollably. My mind raced through horrible scenarios. My heart felt on the verge of exploding. A part of me wanted them to hurry up and tell me the horrible news . . . yet another part of me thought, no please don't. Do not make this real! I will never forget the look in the eyes of the police officer who extended his hand towards me. I pulled away, shaking my head in denial. And then it came. The words I could not bear to hear. "I'm sorry. Your son, Tyler, was found deceased this morning in his bed by his roommate." There are no words to describe this pain. I screamed "NOOOOO!!!" My legs went out from under me, but someone already had a chair ready for me. I thought I would vomit. I sat frozen, body shaking—my mind trying to absorb those words. No, not my son. This happens to other people—not to me. Not my boy. The officer went on to say, "There were no signs of violence or suicide." I nodded, wondering if this should make me feel better. In a strange way, it did. He went on to give me instructions that my mind could not grasp. "He's been taken to the medical examiner's office in Calgary and will remain there until they can perform the autopsy. Here's a card with the name and phone number of the examiner. You can call them to arrange to have his body brought back to Camrose." I nodded as if I understood, but my mind was in a haze. "Our volunteers can drive you home," I heard him say. How could I even manage the simple task of walking out the front door? "I need my husband," were the only words I could choke out.

Jeff is my third husband. We met when my boys were in their teens. I'd wondered how he would adjust from single life to married with teenagers, but I knew we'd figure it out. Jeff and I are good together, and my world feels stable with him in it. He is a man of his word—someone who protects me and takes care of me. And in that moment, more than ever, I needed him to take care of me.

The police officers offered to drive me to his workplace. But first, I needed to tell Alan and Grant. Without knowing any details, they knew it was bad. The police officer brought them into the office where I sat, still trembling—my tears replaced by shock. Grant kneeled on one side of me and Alan on the other, each with one hand on my arms. "Tyler is dead." I said the words, but it did not seem real. Grant broke down, and I told him, "I'll be ok." What a strange thing for me to say. I had never been further from ok. I told them I was going home and didn't know when I would return. "Of course," they said. "Whatever you need, we're here for you."

The Victim Services volunteers drove me to Jeff's workplace just a few blocks away. It felt like an eternity. As I walked into the building, I noticed how strange it felt to be walking. I was aware of my legs propelling me forward, but yet I was numb. Each step took such effort. Jeff was in the hallway and smiled when he saw me. As quickly as his smile came, it left. He saw my face and knew something was very wrong. Collapsing into his arms, I sobbed, "Tyler is gone."

We drove home together, followed by the police and Victim Services volunteers. They sat with us for a while, doing their best to console. Then, they left us alone to grieve. While I couldn't bear to inflict this horrendous news on anyone else, I had no choice. It was time to start contacting family and friends. Tyler's younger brother, Jordan, had to be first.

Tyler and Jordan were opposite in so many ways, but despite their differences, they shared a deep bond. When they were toddlers, I could put a few toys in front of Jordan, and he would play happily for hours. But I didn't dare take my eyes off Tyler because if there was trouble to be found, he'd find it. As an adult, he would laugh when I told him stories of his childhood antics. In jest I'd say, "Just wait until you have kids. It won't be funny then!" Jordan was a quiet introvert, Tyler a raging extrovert, yet they were inseparable growing up. Tyler played the big brother role well and was very protective of Jordan. They didn't fight verbally or physically. If Jordan was sad that Tyler went off to play with friends, Tyler would say, "He can come with us if he wants, Mom." And happily, they'd scamper off. Tyler's friends knew that if they invited Tyler over to play, chances were Jordan would be there too. They were a package deal—that's just the way it was. As adults, they drifted in different directions. They didn't see each other much, but when they were together, the bond was as deep as ever. They would talk about work, friends, and girls. They played games together and laughed just like they did as youngsters. Those were the moments when life felt complete and my heart would sing. And now I had to tell Jordan that his only brother—the brother he loved so deeply—was gone.

Jordan lived in the same city as us, but often his work took him out of town. How would we track him down and get him home without alarming him? Jeff called Jordan's employer and asked where he was working that day. He was in town and had the day off. This was rare, and we were thankful. I couldn't let him hear my voice. Instead, I sent him a text asking him to stop by the house. Within a few minutes, my phone dinged. "Sure, I'm out running errands, so I'll pop by in 10 or 15 minutes." Jeff and I sat on the couch together in silence as we waited. How cruel life seemed at that moment. I had lost one son. Now, I had to deliver news that would devastate my other son. I hated that I had to do this. Anxiety choked me when I heard his car. He walked through the door, saw our faces, and said nothing more than "What?" Instantly he knew something was wrong. I went to him, hugged him, and then . . . I told him. There were no more words. We just held each other and cried.

There were four more people who had to hear this news from me. Then, Jeff could take over. First was James, Tyler's biological dad. We had divorced over 20 years ago with little connection since. I knew from the beginning that we weren't right for each other, but my desire to marry and start a family had overshadowed my doubts.

After the marriage ended, James developed multiple sclerosis and also battled mental health issues. I knew James would need his family by his side when he heard the news, so I called his sister, Tina. Although I hadn't been part of their family for over 20 years, my love and respect for her had never faded. I knew I could lean on her. Again, I choked out the awful news: "Tyler died last night." She was at a loss for words, but I still felt her love and support through that phone line. I knew she'd find the best way to tell James he had lost a son, and for that I was grateful.

Mason, my second husband, was next. We met when Tyler was four and Jordan was one. We were very different. I still wonder why we ever dated, never mind married. But I believe our lives were meant to cross—some part of me needed him, and I also held a special place in his life journey. Together with his son, Michael, our family of five made great memories. Mason knew the art of playing, and he played like there was no place in the world he'd rather be. He loved watching the boys transform our living room into a secret fort. For hours on end, they'd play army with nothing more than a bucket of plastic soldiers and a ton of imagination. And Lego—what they would create simply amazed me. Board games were always a big part of our family fun time. The first game the boys fell in love with was *Trouble*. And just like baths and bedtime stories, that game became part of our nightly routine. As the boys grew older, our tradition evolved, and the strategic game of *Risk* became our family's Sunday afternoon pastime.

Despite our differences, I admired how he loved my boys. I often joked that Mason married me for my children. It broke my heart to tell him Tyler was gone—to hear him cry as I had done only hours before.

Next was "my girl" Cassie. I'm not sure when she received this pet name from me, but it felt right. Maybe our souls were connected in another lifetime. I remember the day we first met. Tyler and Cassie had just started dating, and Tyler was ready to introduce us. I was excited to meet her, so I made the drive to the small town in northern Alberta where they were living. We made arrangements to meet at a local coffee shop for lunch. Tyler and I arrived first. We chatted as we waited for Cassie to arrive. When she walked in, she had a radiance that lit up the room. She extended her hand and said, "Hi, I'm Cassie." I felt an instant connection. Years later, I would learn that she felt the same. We had a nice visit, and the next day when I returned home, Tyler called to ask me what I thought of her. "Your opinion means a lot to me, Mom," I remember him saying. I loved hearing those words because growing up Tyler was quick to dismiss my advice. I smiled and said, "This girl is special." I wonder now if Tyler brought her to me because his soul knew we'd need each other one day.

I hated dialling her number. She answered. After a pause, I said those terrible words again. She screamed and ran from the phone. I was grateful her mom was there to give her the hugs that I could not.

Each conversation took immense emotional energy. I had nothing left, but I needed to find the strength for one more. I had to tell my mother that she had lost a grandson. She lived alone, and I knew she would need us there. Jeff, Jordan, and I made the half-hour drive to her little apartment. When she saw us, she said, "This can't be good." This time it was Jeff who spoke those words. I felt numb—my pain replaced by shock. I was an empty shell who didn't resemble the person I'd been only hours before. This was the beginning of the cycle of emotions that would take over my world. Pain ... numbness ... pain ... numbness ...

I was anxious to get home. Home would feel safe. Jeff made more calls to friends and family. When they asked, "How's Michele?" Jeff answered, "Not very good." Some asked to talk to me, but I just couldn't. Exhausted, I collapsed into my bed and thought of Tyler who would not be in his bed tonight. I cried for him as I drifted off to sleep.

2

MY LONGEST DAYS

SATURDAY – Of all the horrendous moments I would endure over the months ahead, waking up that first morning after Tyler's passing was the worst. Before my eyes opened to the light of day, tears streamed down my cheeks. Everything about the previous day seemed surreal. Tyler was gone. He had died, and I would never see him again. How could this be? Why was I denied the chance to say goodbye and to hug him one last time? It wasn't fair.

Jeff woke in the same moment. He pulled me close as I released uncontrollable sobs. I'm sure his big burly arms were the only things holding me together at that moment.

Nothing prepared me for this pain—not just the emotional pain, but the physical pain. Getting out of bed was a monumental task. The short walk from the bedroom to the living room was exhausting. All I could do was exist.

It was mid-morning when we heard a sound outside. Jeff looked out to see Alan shovelling our driveway. Despite being springtime, a light snow had fallen during the night. Jeff called him to the door so we could thank him. "I had to do something," he replied. The events of yesterday weighed heavy on him too. His thoughtfulness touched us deeply.

I do not have a big network of friends, but the ones I do have are real gems. And among all my gems, Lynda is the diamond that shines the brightest. She has always been there for me, and at that moment, she knew exactly what I needed. She quickly put together a coordinated meal plan, scheduling someone from our network of friends to stop by each evening with dinner. I was barely able to function and to cook a meal would have been unthinkable. Their kindness meant the world to me.

The first meal that arrived was a pot of chili with homemade buns. I didn't realize how hungry I was until I smelled the wonderful aroma. Chili and buns—what a perfect comfort meal. I took a big spoonful of chili and said to Jeff, "This is delicious." But as soon as those words were out of my mouth, I was overcome with guilt. Here I was enjoying a home-cooked meal when my son was dead. How dare I allow myself pleasure at something he could never again experience.

Somehow, I survived that first day on earth knowing that Tyler was not. It was the longest day of my life.

SUNDAY – This was the day we met with the funeral home. On our way there, I saw a mom walking to the park with her two little boys. This was a normal everyday occurrence— one that I would hardly notice. But on this day, it brought a wave of intense grief. I clasped my hands over my chest as I cried. It was the first of many unexpected triggers. To someone who has not experienced loss, this might not seem rational. But I would soon learn there was nothing logical or predicable about this journey.

Intellectually, I knew that trips to the playground had not suddenly been taken from me. My son had been an adult, after all. But everywhere I looked, I saw reminders of the life that once was—the one that had been ruthlessly stripped away from me.

Everything seemed surreal as we drove into the parking lot of the funeral home. I leaned heavily on Jeff's arm as we walked towards the entrance. Jordan met us there. One of the funeral directors greeted us with kind condolences and led us into a quiet room. Despite how carefully he spoke, the questions came too quickly. How many do you expect for the service . . . burial or cremation . . . who will be pallbearers . . . who will perform the service . . . open or closed casket . . . do you want a memorial service the night before . . . would you like us to create a memory video . . . my mind was spinning. I tried my best to answer the questions, but I wanted to scream, "I should not be here!"

We left with the list of tasks we'd been asked to complete. I needed to get home so I could collapse into my grief in the safety of our home.

MONDAY – The medical examiner's office released Tyler's body. He would be brought back to Camrose to the funeral home. Mason wanted to drive to Calgary to follow him home. "You don't have to do that," I told him. "I **need** to do this," was his reply. I understood. I was anxious for Tyler to return. I can't explain why. I just needed to know he was back home.

I asked Mason if he would pick up Tyler's clothes while he was in Calgary. I know it took every ounce of strength for him to do this, and for that I'm forever grateful.

I went to the flower shop to pick out a spray for the casket. They gave me a book to look through. I flipped through the pages and then pointed to one on the last page. It's not that I liked it best. I just didn't care. It felt meaningless.

I resented having to buy a dress for the service. After trying on a few, I found one that seemed right. The saleslady said, "You'll be able to wear it again." I wanted to slap her. Instead, I paid for the dress and left. I've never returned to that store since.

Jordan needed a new dress shirt for the service. As he tried on shirts, I slid to the floor and sat outside his dressing room. I didn't care if I looked odd. What little strength I had was gone.

Cassie was able to get a flight back to Alberta. At the time of Tyler's passing, she was living in her small hometown in Ontario. I heard a car pull up. I cried as I saw her walking up the sidewalk. It was good to have her there with us. We hugged tightly and cried together.

TUESDAY – I needed to decide what Tyler should wear for his final ensemble. It was fun picking his outfits together when he was a wee boy. But on this day, it devastated me. Mason brought over the box of clothes he had picked up the day prior. As I watched him walk up our front steps, carrying this precious box in his trembling hands, I crumbled. Reality hit—this was all I had left of my boy. Gently, he placed the box on the floor. We wrapped our arms around each other forming a group hug—Jeff, Mason, Cassie, Jordan, and me—bound together by our mutual love for Tyler.

We took the box of clothes downstairs and sat together in his old bedroom. It always stayed "Tyler's room," even after he moved away. Strange that Jordan's room was quickly converted to an office. Deep down, perhaps I knew it would be important to keep a special place in our home that would always be Tyler's.

Tenderly, I opened the box and caressed the shirts. Silently, I thanked whoever had taken such care to neatly fold each item. I pulled out a light grey sweatshirt and clasped it tightly to my heart. The memory of hugging him when he wore it washed over me. How I yearned to be hugging him in that moment.

Each piece of clothing brought a memory. We shared. We cried. Then, the decision was easy. Jeans of course, a bit tatty, a hoodie with the sleeves pushed up just a little, his belt, a lanyard hanging out of his pocket, his watch, along with the silver chain he wore always, hat and sunglasses beside him. Yes, that was my Tyler—perfectly him.

It was also on this day that I sat at my kitchen table, tasked with writing my son's obituary—a task I never dreamed I'd have to do. The funeral home gave me some samples from recent services. As I looked through them, I was filled with anger. These are old people, I thought. They had lived long lives. How on earth could this help me write something for my 25-year-old son who should have had a lifetime ahead of him? I put everything aside and opened my heart.

Tyler was born in Wetaskiwin on April 10, 1990, first son to proud parents James and Michele. Tyler was full of life and energy from the moment he came into this world. On December 21, 1992, Tyler became a big brother to Jordan. He was a loving and caring brother, always happy to have his little brother tagging along. Very unusual for brothers, but these two never fought. They were each other's best friend. In 1997, a new stepbrother (Michael) and stepdad (Mason) came into his life. Together we shared so many wonderful family memories that we will forever hold close to our hearts.

Looking for an outlet for Tyler's endless energy, he became involved in sports at a young age—first hockey and later soccer. In his early teens, Tyler travelled to Europe with his soccer team for a once-in-a-lifetime experience. When Tyler wasn't at the hockey rink or on the soccer field, you might find him playing Halo or StarCraft with his buddies, pulling out the Risk board for a family Sunday afternoon as became our tradition, or trying to learn a new trick on his skateboard.

After high school, Tyler began working on a service rig. He loved to work hard and get his hands dirty.

A few years later, he met his love, Cassie. Their love weathered the storms and was undying. Even when distance separated them, their love endured.

Tyler moved to Calgary in December 2014 and was excited about a fresh new start in his life. He started doing some construction work and loved learning new skills. Tyler fell in love with Calgary and the surrounding area, and he was always excited to tell us about his outings and new discoveries. We find great peace in remembering these last few months and having the opportunity to share in Tyler's excitement for life and the future.

Tyler was an outgoing young man who loved meeting new people and always surrounded himself with friends.

He loved the outdoors, hiking and fishing, and just being with friends.

Tyler left us peacefully on April 24th close to friends he called his brotherhood.

The poem for the back of his obituary pamphlet was not one I picked from a book. Instead, I wrote this personal note to my boy:

Taken too soon. So hard to comprehend why. Not for us to understand yet. My life was blessed when you came into this world 25 short years ago. To hear your first words, watch you take your first steps, tuck you into bed at night, snuggle you close, and watch you grow into an amazing young man . . . these are the memories I will forever hold close to my heart. Remember when we were talking a few months ago, I said I believed there was a guardian angel watching over you. I truly believe that, and now that angel is keeping you safe. I don't understand yet why your angel had to take you so soon, but I know there is a reason. Someday I will find peace with this, just not yet. For today, know you are loved more than anything in this life. Rest peacefully now, my boy— my dear, sweet Tyler.

Love you forever,

Mom

As a family, we put together our favourite memories for the pastor to read as part of the service. These memories and stories perfectly personified all that Tyler was.

FROM JEFF:

Ty, you always had so much energy and passion for the things that you loved. Whether it was talking hockey— you especially loved telling me how great the Leafs were 'cause you knew I hated them; or whether it was playing games—your Farkle strategy was: just keep rollin' the dice, win big, or go home; or whether it was telling me about Game of Thrones—"Ah dude, you gotta watch that" (and I did start watching it, and you got me hooked!!!); or whether it was a new start on life, you did everything with all-out passion. But none more so than loving your family and friends. You have touched an incredible amount of people in your life, and when I hugged you and told you that I was proud of you, I meant it and still do! Rest in peace, Tyler.

FROM CASSIE:

We went to Niagara Falls last summer and this crazy guy . . . we went on Maid of the Mist and let me tell you, you get wet no matter what . . . but that wasn't enough for Ty Guy. He takes his raincoat off and goes right to the front of the boat. He wanted to get misted to the max, and oh he did! Ty, you're my number one and always will be babe. I thought I missed you before when distance was our only hurdle, but this is a whole new ball game. I will never stop loving you! Please wait for me and your loved ones on the other side. I know this isn't goodbye— it's see you later.

FROM GRANDMA:

One of my fondest memories is watching Tyler learn to play hockey. He was so little and couldn't skate. But he was determined, and with all his might, he propelled himself clumsily forward. And then he couldn't stop, so "bam" into the boards he would go. I always looked forward to sitting at the rink and watching him play hockey—a memory I will always hold close to my heart.

FROM JORDAN:

Tyler was always pushing me and challenging me in ways only a brother could—whether it was practicing soccer in the backyard or teaching me to do kickflips on the skateboard, he always wanted to help me get better. After he mastered the kickflip, I didn't even need to ask him—he showed me and taught me how to do it as well. We had so many fun times at the Red Deer outdoor swimming pool. He was the sole reason I jumped off the 15-foot diving board. At the time, I was so scared, but Tyler calmed me down and made it easier. He gave me a tip: "Point your feet down, or else the soles of your feet will hurt when they hit the water." The moment my feet left the board, I forgot everything he told me, and my feet sure did hurt! Years later, jumping off boats and cliffs in Thailand, I was using that advice without really thinking about where I had learned it. He taught me more than I realized before this day and I'm so grateful that I had him as a big brother. I will always push myself to be better and do things to the best of my ability, just like he always did. You will always be by my side, Tyler, challenging me.

FROM ME:

That crazy hair he was born with, and the first thing anyone said when they saw our precious new baby . . . look at all that hair!

Countless hours tying skates at the hockey rink and how proud he was to become a goalie.

How crazy good he was with numbers—he could add anything in his head.

Connection with his soccer team buddies here in Camrose. Many hours on the field. All those bottle drives to raise money for the team's trip to Europe.

The hours we spent at the kitchen table playing Risk as a family. Those games went on for hours and sometimes into the next day.

Making chocolate snowballs for Christmas together.

Our first trip to Mexico together—just me and my boys. Such a special memory.

His hugs—his big, strong arms around me. He was a great hugger. Hugged like he really meant it. Warmed me to my core every time.

Never being afraid to say, "I love you" whenever we talked, no matter where he was or who he was around.

This day, and the days leading up to this day, were consumed with planning his service—his Celebration of Life. As any mother knows, your heart changes the day you are blessed with a child. Without sacrifice, you quickly give up expensive vacations, fancy clothes, and dinners out because you find far more pleasure in buying your child that new pair of sneakers that are the latest rage or the latest video game they are desperate to have. Nothing warms your heart more than a smile on your child's face. Planning this service would be my last motherly gift. And if this was the last thing I would give to my son, I was going to make him proud. I wanted to feel him smile down on us.

I wanted the service to feel like "him," but some parts were just for me—to bring me comfort. The opening song of "The Prayer" by Josh Groban and Celine Dion—that was for me. But "See You Again" by Wiz Khalifa—that one was all Tyler. Just a few weeks before, Tyler went to see the movie, *Fast & Furious 7*. He was so impacted by this song that he felt compelled to call me as he was walking out of the theatre. He told me how it brought a tear to his eye. Unusual, I thought. Not that Tyler wasn't sentimental, but just how much it touched him seemed out of character. When he got home, he posted the link to the YouTube video on his Facebook page. I now wonder if his soul knew this would be his song.

I asked Mason if he would say the eulogy. Initially he said, "I'd love to, but there is no way I could get through it." Like me, he was just too broken. But every day brought a little more healing. Days before the service, he called to tell me he had found the strength he needed and would like the honour of delivering Tyler's eulogy. I knew he'd find exactly the right words, and that he did.

Thank you all for coming today to share in our grief and to help us celebrate the life of a remarkable young man.

Tyler came into my life when he was four. He and Jordan stole my heart and thus began the best years any life could be blessed with. With each passing day, we grew closer, learned from each other, and created such amazing memories. Though life holds many ups and downs, I know for a fact that there is nothing that will compare to the joy you two brought to my life. I know that now and for the rest of my life I can reflect on that joy with a smile, with a tear, and with a laugh.

For anyone who was lucky enough to get a hug from Tyler, you know they were special. I can still feel Tyler's last hug. Like every hug, it was 110% and embraced your heart to the very core. My God, could that boy hug! But that was Tyler whether it was work, play, or love, it was 110%. We could all take a lesson from that. Our grief in his passing is inevitable. Clearly his life ended far too soon. But Tyler would not accept just grief. A celebration of his life is what he would want, so that is what we must do. As the sadness begins to ebb away, it leaves us with the joy he brought to our lives. Nothing can take that away. That is Tyler's gift to us all, and it is everlasting.

Thank you, Michele and James, for bringing such an amazing person into our world and our hearts. Michele, your strength this last week has helped me move through these dark days. I cannot thank you enough. You are an amazing person. Thank you all for your support. Your words, your thoughts, and your presence has helped us through the grief.

WEDNESDAY – A day of waiting—nothing left to do but wait. The day the family would see Tyler for private goodbyes before the following day's public ceremony. When we arrived at the funeral home, other family members were already standing outside. We supported each other as we made our way inside. We sat in the pews for a few moments, preparing ourselves. But nothing can prepare a mom to see her son this way. The funeral director invited us into the private room where Tyler had been laid so carefully in the casket we had picked for him. With trepidation, we stepped into the room . . . and then I saw him. Jeff was there to catch me as I broke. We took turns hugging and supporting each other. Through his broken cries, Mason said, "He looks so peaceful." He was right. While we emanated agony, Tyler radiated peace.

THURSDAY – The day we would say our goodbyes and celebrate the life lived by my son, Tyler. The minutes felt like hours. We paced. We sat in silence in our own emotional space—the air heavy, the silence deafening. Cassie and I painted our toenails black with one in red—Tyler's favourite colours. He would've liked this. Time to get dressed. Cassie wondered which shoes to wear. The black heels, I suggested. Even on this day, she looked pretty. Jeff helped Jordan tie his tie. It should've been for a happier occasion. My stomach was in knots.

12:00 P.M. – Time to go. One last group hug before we walked out the door. We drove in silence. I'm living my worst nightmare, I thought. We made our way inside the church to the family room. This was meant to be our safe place, but somehow it did not feel safe. Nothing about today seemed real—it was simply too much to comprehend. Suddenly, I realized it was 1:00 p.m.—time for the service to begin. NO, I'm not ready! NOT YET! Panic set in. I could not bear the thought of them closing the casket, knowing I would never see him again. "Please give me just a few more minutes," I pleaded. With no one else in sight, I stood by his casket—just me and my boy. I cried as I gently stroked his cheek, telling him how much I loved him and how proud I was to be his mom.

1:00 p.m. – It was time. "All rise." With arms wrapped around each other, we followed Tyler's casket down the aisle. Even with my eyes lowered, I knew the pews were filled. I was in awe of all the people who came to support us and share in our love for Tyler. I could feel their love, and it gave me strength—strength to walk down that aisle following my son's casket. One foot . . . then the next . . . slowly we made our way to the front pews reserved just for us.

We sat together tightly, listening to the beautiful words and stories. I clung to every word. I heard the sobs around me and wanted to comfort those who hurt, just as I hurt. And then . . . the service ended. I wanted to stay locked in that moment surrounded by love. I wasn't ready to see them carry away his casket. Don't take my boy! But I had no choice. I followed as they carried him away . . . watched as they lifted him into the hearse . . . I could not contain the primal cries of my grief as they slowly drove away. My boy was gone.

3

BEFORE & AFTER

In the days, weeks, and months following Tyler's passing, I felt every emotion imaginable more intensely than ever before. I felt pain, sadness, depression, anger, guilt, but most of all, I felt broken. The heaviness in my heart never left me. I tried to disguise it under the smiles that were nothing more than a mask I forced myself to wear. I was certain that the days of belly laughs and giddy excitement were part of my past. I didn't wallow in self-pity at the loss of this part of myself. I simply accepted that I had changed.

Panic attacks became familiar. They came without warning. Anxiety would swell up inside, suffocating me. I was fearful of when the next attack would hit. At first, I fought them. My insides screaming, no, no, no . . . please not again! But anxiety was impervious to my pleas. As much as I hated these attacks, they were part of my grieving journey. With every attack I allowed myself to experience, the intensity decreased and my fear lessened. Breathe, just breathe, I'd say to myself. Slowly it would pass and my breathing would return to a steady rhythm. I learned that the only way to heal was to walk through the pain. I could not stuff it down or go around it; there was no avoiding it. Straight through was the only path to finding my peace.

Perhaps it was a form of PTSD (post-traumatic stress disorder). I relived every moment—every emotion—a million times . . . the words of the police officer, the shock, the pain ripping through me, watching those I love hurt as deeply as me, images of him in a casket, the songs at his funeral . . . I couldn't turn it off. Sometimes this was ok. Other times, I wanted so badly to turn off the recording that played over and over in my mind. But no matter what I was doing or who I was with, grief never left me. I wondered if it ever would.

My life was divided into two distinct halves: *before* and *after.* Everything landed in one bucket or the other. I'd walk into a store and think, "This is the first time I've been here in the *after* part of my life" or "this is the first time I've seen so and so" or "I haven't been to this restaurant since." Every experience, no matter how trivial, felt like a first.

I remember the first time I greeted a stranger with a "good morning" where my smile was real and I truly meant those two simple words. In my life *after,* I would utter "good morning" as an obligatory gesture. But inside, I was bitter and hated these happy exchanges. That day was different—a sliver of peace trickled into my heart. I was walking down a beautiful trail that was so quiet and serene. Tall trees loomed over me, casting a light shadow, and the morning sun peeked through the branches. The air was crisp from a light rain the night before. I couldn't help but feel gratitude for this beautiful morning. A man walking towards me smiled. Without having to force myself, I smiled back. "Good morning."

The words came out so naturally, without thinking. Hearing the words escape my lips, I knew my heart had healed a tiny bit.

I quickly became overwhelmed by situations that *before* never fazed me. Public settings were challenging. I could never predict what would trigger me, bringing tears without warning. I sought refuge in my home where no one could witness my sudden waves of grief. My cocoon was comfortable, but I knew it wasn't healthy to hide. Vowing to leave the house every day, I became intentional about reconnecting with the outside world. Each day, I picked a public place to visit—sometimes only for a few minutes and other times longer. These outings felt like workouts, not unlike my previous training runs. But I was no longer training for race day. Now, it was for a transition to reality—to a life I once knew *before*.

After, the trivial chore of grocery shopping was unexpectedly overwhelming, bringing a flood of anxiety and emotion. I started slowly, purchasing just a few necessities on my first outing. I can't say why I felt so challenged by this task. Was it the eyes of strangers? It felt like they were looking straight into my soul, seeing my wounds and wondering, "Gee, I wonder what happened to her?" Or was it the flood of memories as I turned down every aisle? Chicken noodle soup—oh how he loved chicken noodle soup. Even after he left home, I always kept a couple of cans in my cupboard. Only my Tyler would have chicken noodle soup on his list of favourite snacks! And then there were beans—his most dreaded food. Tyler wasn't a fussy eater. He would eat almost anything, except beans! It became a little joke in our household. I could almost hear his voice, "Ughhh Mom, why did you put beans in the chili?" Mini-Wheats—his all-time favourite cereal growing up. He couldn't possibly start his day without them! Nachos—a favourite Saturday afternoon snack. I could almost hear his squeals of delight, "Yayyy, nachos!" Popcorn—a reminder of family movie nights. Everywhere were memories. I tried to keep my tears in check, but sometimes I just couldn't. Gathering my groceries was hard enough, but then there was the dreaded checkout process. The inevitable "Hi, how are you today?" was a dagger through my heart. I did my best to choke out "Fine," hoping the cashier wouldn't engage in small talk. Then almost done, bracing myself for the cashier's cheery parting comment, "You have a nice day now." I hated those words.

I dreaded special occasions . . . birthdays, Mother's Day, Christmas . . . all painful reminders of our changed lives. Tyler turned 25 just two weeks before he died. I told him I'd cook him a nice dinner next time he was home. If I'd only known . . .

It was difficult to listen to friends engage in small talk about their families. I wanted to feel happy for them, but resentment would rise up in me. Why did they get to have their family intact? It wasn't fair. I'd look for an excuse to walk away or change the subject. When I was forced to listen, I'd smile and say the appropriate words, but it was fake. Inside I was angry that our family had changed when everyone else's hadn't.

About a month after Tyler's passing, my mom turned 70. Normally, this would be a milestone to celebrate, but that year it was endured. Ugly feelings surfaced that I'm not proud of. I wanted a trade. If grief had to strike our family, why couldn't God have chosen her instead? I'd still be grieving, but acceptance would have been easier.

Then, there was my birthday. I hated my first birthday in

my life *after* Tyler. I hated that I wouldn't hear my phone ding with his text. I hated that I wouldn't hear him say, "Hey! Happy Birthday, Mom." I hated that I'd outlived my son.

Mother's Day – When you lose a child, your identity is shaken. I was still a mom, but was I a mom of one son or two? When someone asks me how many children I have, how should I answer? In my heart, I'd always be a mother of two, but is that how I should identify myself? Would it be uncomfortable for the other person when they learned one of my sons had died? In the end, I decided it didn't matter how it felt for others—it had to feel right for me. I'll always be a proud mom of two sons.

Christmas – How I dreaded our first Christmas. Christmas gatherings for our family were small—Jeff and myself, Tyler and Cassie, Jordan, and my mom. Tyler brought energy to our house, and I couldn't imagine the day without him. I needed it to be completely different. It's the only way I would survive it. So, I reserved a little chalet in the mountains—something we'd never done before. I thought getting away from home would make it easier. But as the day got closer, I realized grief would follow. Knowing there was no refuge, I cancelled our reservations. I tried to make it an ordinary day without any triggers. I didn't cook our traditional dinner. Instead, I made waffles. What could be more ordinary than waffles? We all played this little charade of pretending we were ok. But we weren't. Even without a tree in our living room or turkey on our dinner table, it was still our first Christmas without Tyler. I was reminded again that the only way to heal was to walk through the pain. I dug through my cupboards and found four tea lights. I placed one beside each place setting and said, "Now we will remember Tyler." I lit my candle first and then passed the lighter to Jeff. Everyone had their turn, lighting their special candle and silently remembering. Finally, the charade was over, and together we cried.

April 24, 2016. – The one-year anniversary of Tyler's passing. I'd made it. I'd survived all the firsts. I thought this would end my grieving period, only to learn there was no finish line.

Before, I'd heard of Kübler-Ross and the five stages of grief model. This model seemed logical. I assumed I would start at stage one: denial, and after spending some time here, I'd move to stage two: anger and so on. I'd know exactly where I was and could gauge if I got stuck along the way. Not so at all. Nothing I was feeling fit neatly into boxes, nor was there any logical pattern. Denial, anger, bargaining, depression, acceptance—if only the journey was that simple.

If I'd designed the stages of grief, I would have added a sixth stage: guilt. It turned my stomach inside out and came at me from so many directions.

"Survivor guilt is a mental condition that occurs when a person believes they have done wrong by surviving a traumatic event when others did not" (Wikipedia). This definition fit perfectly. I'd outlived my child and that was wrong—so unnatural. I felt guilty for just being, for waking each morning, for every breath, and for every experience.

A few days after Tyler's death, I stepped out onto our back deck. The sun was shining; it was a perfect spring day. I closed my eyes and tilted my head towards the sky, relishing in the warmth of the sun. But my pleasure was quickly replaced by guilt. What kind of mother sits outside enjoying the beautiful sunshine when her son is dead! Repulsed that I had allowed myself that brief moment of enjoyment, I went back inside.

I felt guilty for being healthy. I despised my strong, healthy body, knowing I likely had 30 or 40 years of life without my son. The fact that I'd been given the gift of good health when Tyler didn't have even one more breath felt very wrong. Everything was backwards.

I felt guilty for things said and for things unsaid. Tyler and I shared a close bond, but sometimes our relationship was difficult. We were wired differently—Tyler, the freewheeler; me, the disciplined rule follower. Despite the many times I told him I loved him and was proud of who he was, there were just as many when I told him he could do better or try harder. In the last year of his life, he told me, "I wish I could be more like you, Mom." It devastated me. I thought he liked being a bit of a badass rebel, living life with reckless enthusiasm and never worrying about tomorrow. Now, I saw that part of him longed to be different. For the first time, I realized choices that seemed so simple to me were much more difficult for him. Had I pushed him to be someone he simply couldn't be?

Then, there was the big ugly guilt—the one that almost ate me alive. While aimlessly surfing the internet just weeks before Tyler's passing, I stumbled across an article on fentanyl. I read how deadly it was: 80 times more powerful than morphine and hundreds of times more powerful than heroin. As I read the statistics on the number of young lives that had been taken by this deadly drug, a shiver went through me . . . a premonition maybe. I needed to share this with Tyler and tell him to be careful—that he wasn't invincible. We had plans to meet for dinner the following week, so I printed the article and put it in my car so I wouldn't forget it.

I picked him up excited, as always, to see him. The conversation was ordinary—nothing significant. Then, he said something (I can't even remember what it was) that launched me into a tirade of unsolicited motherly advice. The conversation lost its comfortable tone. I could tell he felt deflated, like he had fallen short of my expectations yet again. I felt terrible, but it was too late to take back my words.

As we drove back, he was quiet and solemn. I tried to lighten the mood, but to no avail. Solemnly, he gave me a big hug—one that lasted a little longer than usual. There was so much emotion in that hug somehow. It left me feeling unsettled.

After sitting quietly in my car for a few minutes, thinking about the events of the evening, I looked behind me before backing out of the parking lot. That's when I saw the neatly folded paper lying on the back seat—the article on fentanyl that I wanted to give him. I thought about going after him, but the night had already taken a downward spiral. Why add fuel to the fire? There would be another time.

A couple of days later, still feeling upset with myself about how our last conversation ended, I thought, I have to talk to Tyler this weekend and make this right. But something niggled inside and told me not wait. That night, I sent Tyler a text, "Nothing in this world means more to me than my boys. You know that right?" He replied, "I know Mom. Love you." With a smile, I texted back, "Love you too and let's talk more this weekend."

This was the last communication I had with my son. That night, he took a tiny blue pill, crawled into bed, and never woke. Fentanyl took his life.

I didn't get to warn him. If I hadn't been so busy "mothering," maybe I would've remembered the article. Maybe if I'd given it to him, he would not have taken that deadly pill. The "what-ifs" consumed me. This was the ultimate guilt; a demon that screamed inside me. I wondered if it would ever let me go.

4

THE HEART KNOWS

My son died of a drug overdose. Long before the autopsy report confirmed it, my heart knew. While Tyler's passing was the most emotionally horrific event of my life, watching him struggle with drug addiction was a close second. Where it started, I can't be sure. Maybe the signs were always there.

Tyler was born with high energy. Even as a baby, napping was infrequent and sleeping through the night was a luxury he did not afford me. His activity level only increased as he learned to walk. He was in constant motion. I tried to read to him, but after a few pages, he'd wiggle off my lap in search of something more exciting. Bedtimes were an ordeal. I'd tuck him in, only to hear the pitter-patter of his little feet sneaking out of bed minutes later. It became our nightly game—an exhausting process, but eventually he would tire and fall asleep.

When he started school, I worried. How would he manage to sit quietly at a desk? But he found ways of coping, like his constant doodling. Still, his favourite time of day was the ringing of the 3:20 p.m. bell so he could be free to play.

Elementary and junior high school went ok. He was a happy, social kid—everyone liked him, including his teachers. With his natural smarts and likeability, he was able to coast along with little effort. During his high school years, things started to slide. Skipping classes became a regular occurrence, and his grades plummeted. It became inevitable that he would not graduate. If it bothered him at all, he did not show it.

This would have been easier for me to accept if he had a plan. But he was drifting aimlessly with no desire to continue his education, no steady job, and no goals for the future. He was smoking marijuana on a regular basis. I hoped this was normal teenage tribulation, but still I worried. When I tried to talk to him about it, he'd tell me I was overreacting. "Everything will work out," he'd say. To appease us, Tyler would hand in the occasional resume. He'd pick up the odd job, but for one reason or another, he never stuck with it.

I worried about depression and urged him to see a doctor. Tyler didn't like the idea, but after much coercion, he agreed. I made the appointment, and we went together. After a brief discussion with us, the doctor seemed rather disinterested and gave him a prescription for antidepressants. Tyler took these pills for a few days. Then, despite my pleas, he stopped. He felt marijuana was a more natural way of dealing with his moods. Feeling helpless, I did nothing, hoping it was a phase that would pass. It didn't.

Tensions rose, and rarely was there a reprieve. The harder I pushed, the more he rebelled. We'd argue in ways that were out of character for us. His personality started to change. He wasn't my happy-go-lucky boy anymore. He seemed angry with the world. I feared that his drug use had escalated from marijuana. When he wasn't working, he'd spend his days in the basement, watching TV or playing video games. At night, he'd go out. Where and with whom, I wasn't certain. His group of friends had changed. I missed his friends I had become so fond of when he was growing up. The friends he had now seemed lost, in much the same way that Tyler was. Jeff and I disagreed on how to handle the situation. Jeff could see the situation objectively, but I was blinded by motherly love. I wanted to ride it out and hope for the best. Jeff wanted to take strong corrective measures. He pushed me to be tougher. I tried, but it wasn't natural for me.

My "wait and hope it gets better" strategy wasn't working. I was in over my head and completely unequipped. Not knowing where to start, I looked up the Alberta Alcohol and Drug Abuse Commission in the phonebook and made an appointment.

I sat nervously in the waiting area, wondering where things went wrong. I like to think I was a good mom—not perfect, but I did all the things a good mom does. I read to the boys when they were little. Volunteered for school field trips. Taught them good morals. Cheered them on at every sporting event. Doesn't this happen in homes where there is already substance abuse? Even in my youth, I never experimented with drugs—it held no appeal. My drinking consisted of a shot of Baileys in my coffee on a cold winter day. Why was I here?

My name was called, jolting me out of my rumination. The counsellor had an easygoing demeanour that put me at ease. I told him my story—probably the same one he'd heard hundreds of times. He listened and was quick to give advice. "Tyler needs clear rules and consequences." I agreed, wondering what he had in mind. He went on to say, "Tonight, you need to tell Tyler he has three weeks to get a job. If he doesn't, he no longer has access to your home and must be told to leave."

"But where would he go?" I asked, shocked by his drastic recommendation. "What if he makes an honest effort to get a job but isn't successful? Wouldn't this consequence be too harsh?" But the counsellor didn't budge. No wiggle room. He told me that Tyler had to know I was serious. I knew I needed to be stronger with Tyler, but the thought of locking him out of his home turned my stomach inside out. This didn't feel like what a supportive mother should do. I wanted to tell him that Tyler was a good kid—that he'd just lost his way. Maybe if he met Tyler he'd see things differently.

That night, I told Jeff about my session and the guidance I'd been given. He urged me to follow through. I knew there was merit in his advice, but I could not bear the thought of it. Surely, there was another way. Jeff was frustrated with my inability to be a firm disciplinarian. I felt torn—should I continue to be the mother I'd always been, the only one I knew how to be, or the one Jeff needed me to be? I wanted so desperately to be unified with my husband. I just couldn't find my way there.

Eager for a second opinion, I called another counsellor. His name was Carl. He was available to meet with Tyler and me the following day. Carl listened to us both with an empathetic ear. I told him of the advice I'd received from a previous counsellor and wanted his opinion. If I was going down that road, I wanted to lay out the rules with Tyler in a neutral environment—one where I'd have support and where Tyler couldn't pull on my heart strings, convincing me that such actions would not be helping him. Sensing my angst and knowing that the likelihood I'd follow through was low, Carl sat for a moment in quiet reflection. Then, he said, "I agree that Tyler needs firmer rules and consequences, but I'd like to suggest another idea. If Tyler agrees to attend weekly counselling sessions with me, would you allow him to live in your home?" With a sigh of relief, I replied, "Yes, I'd agree to that." Then, he turned to Tyler and asked if he could commit to this. Tyler nodded in agreement.

Tyler kept up his end of the deal and met with Carl weekly. Jeff and I also attended our own private sessions. We found some good nuggets of advice in the sessions, but after several months, it felt like we were treading water, keeping our heads just above the surface, but not moving forward. We saw little change in Tyler who continued to rebel against the rules of the home. Jeff and I wanted to be allies and spent countless hours talking, hoping to reach a common ground. But despite our efforts, tensions escalated, and our marriage suffered. While there were hopeful reprieves, the lows were very low. Jeff wanted out of the marriage. This wasn't what he'd bargained for, and I understood. I feared him leaving, but another part of me thought it might be easier. Somehow, we found the strength to continue.

As the months went by, we expressed our concerns and growing frustration to Carl. He told us to be patient. But patience had run out for both of us. Not seeing the change we desperately needed, it was time to change direction again, and we moved onto counsellor #3, Jean, who was a sweet lady with a peaceful presence.

The first session Tyler and I had with Jean was emotionally charged. Skilfully, and in a way that seemed to come so naturally for her, she defused the situation and emotions softened. Tyler and I both felt a connection with her and trust was quickly established. It felt right that Tyler and I were in therapy together—each of us with a voice. Finally, I felt we were on the right path with a perfect combination of the previous two approaches. Counsellor #1 was right—there had to be an ultimatum, but he'd taken me there too quickly. And counsellor #2 knew that love and support had to be part of the plan. But love on its own wasn't solving Tyler's problems.

It was a long, slow process with many ups and downs. Some weeks held so much tension that I'd count the minutes until our next session. We spent countless hours in therapy—Tyler, me, Tyler and me, Jeff and me, all three of us. The combinations were endless, depending on which dynamic was the toughest that week.

In time, things started to shift. Throughout our years of counselling, we all learned something about ourselves. As a parent, I always thought my unconditional love with some gentle guidance would be enough for my boys to feel secure and find their way in the world. For Jordan, this approach worked perfectly. But, despite how much Tyler rebelled against the rules, he needed them. Over time, I learned to establish boundaries. Helping him did not mean owning his problems. I had to let him feel the consequences of his decisions, as hard as that was. I learned to be more direct about my expectations and to refrain from saying anything I couldn't follow through on.

Jeff learned that things aren't always black and white and not everything would go as planned. Sometimes we had to pull ourselves up, forgive the wrongs, and move forward. We all learned to communicate differently, respecting each other even when we didn't agree. It wasn't perfect, but I was proud of how far we'd come.

We had lots to work on, but the primary goal was for Tyler to take ownership of his future. The premise was that if he had a job and adult responsibilities, his interest in drugs would diminish. Tyler's job search efforts increased, and eventually, he landed a job with an oil field company—a job that he was excited about. This felt like the positive catalyst to turn things around. He would be based out of a small town about three hours north. It seemed perfect—just enough distance to make it difficult for me to rescue him and for him to know that he needed to step up and be responsible for his life. I worried about the reputation of oil fields, but my concerns were alleviated by my relief. With change on the horizon, the weight on my shoulders lifted slightly. I hoped that this would be the first of many steps in a positive, new direction.

While many young people are lured to the oil field, most last only a few weeks before realizing they aren't cut out for the long days and rough working conditions. Not Tyler. It was the perfect fit for his high energy, and getting dirty never bothered him. He embraced it all—the long, hard days, harsh weather conditions, "having to prove himself" . . . he never complained. When we talked, I could hear his excitement. He was learning the ropes quickly. He'd proudly tell me that his boss felt he had a lot of potential to move up the ranks. This came as no surprise to me. I began to feel that maybe all the troubles of the past were behind us. Tyler was happy again, and we re-established our bond.

About a year later, Tyler started dating Cassie. She wasn't his first serious girlfriend, but I had a feeling that she might be "the one."

Tyler's first love was Amanda—his high school sweetheart. He was so taken with her that he became a vegetarian for a while, just because she was. While we were enjoying hamburgers, he'd tell us with conviction that his vegan burger was delicious! Amanda was a sweet girl, but the relationship wasn't meant to be. Tyler did everything with intensity, including loving deeply. When they broke up, he was devastated. I knew Amanda would always hold a special place in his heart.

Tyler's next serious girlfriend was Jess. They stated dating shortly before Tyler moved north. She loved him enough to follow him there. They lived together and worked on "adulting." When we'd go visit, their place was spick and span, with the smell of fragrant candles in the air. We'd share a nice meal together, and the conversation was comfortable. I was proud of their efforts. But soon real-world realities set in, and the relationship deteriorated. And again, Tyler was left heartbroken.

After the breakup with Jess, Tyler announced that he was done with girls. But I knew better. Tyler liked being in a relationship. I knew it wouldn't be long before he found a new love. That special girl was Cassie, and oh, how he loved that girl. With a job that he enjoyed and a girl he cared about, I thought for sure that his life would only get better.

The next couple of years were good. Tyler and Cassie came home on weekends when their work schedules allowed it, and our family grew from four to five. He continued to love his job and had moved up to the position of derrick hand. He wanted to become a driller, and he seemed to be on his way. From my vantage point, everything looked positive. I had no apparent reason to worry, yet I could never completely let my guard down.

Then, things changed. Tyler and Cassie started fighting—but not the little squabbles that every relationship endures. These were big blow-ups. The passion that fuelled their love now ignited their fights. After a year of heated arguments, breakups, and makeups, they agreed that they both needed to get healthy for their relationship to work. Tyler encouraged Cassie to go home to her family in Ontario so she could be in a better environment. "She needs to get out of this place," he told me. Tyler made it sound like Cassie was the one who'd lost her way, but I would later learn it was Tyler who'd become entrenched in a world of darkness.

Tyler and Cassie parted as friends. Cassie went home, found a good job, and slowly started to get herself on the right path. With Cassie gone, Tyler was on shaky ground. Either he'd find the strength to pull himself out or he'd sink. I prayed for the former, but that prayer wasn't answered. Things went from bad to worse, and the year ahead was sheer hell.

5

FINDING HOPE

I could never admit that Tyler struggled with addiction. I just didn't see him that way. Through my eyes, he was always my happy, outgoing boy. Maybe I was too proud to admit it. Addiction didn't belong in our family, but deep down I knew it was there.

My barometer was that as long as he had work and a roof over his head, he was doing ok. But when he called, crying hysterically, to tell me he'd lost his job, I knew. Drugs had taken control. My fears—the ones I had buried deep—were real. I could no longer pretend everything was ok. Cocaine and opiates had become his daily crutch.

Tyler was scared. His life was spinning out of control, but he could not stop. I hated to see him hurting and hoped this would be his bottom—the point when he could no longer deny that drugs were negatively impacting his life. Surely now, he would be jolted into action. But it would take more than this for Tyler to reach rock bottom.

Months after losing his job, he was evicted from his townhouse.

It was inevitable. No job, no money—another devastating result. I was scared. Where would he go? But a friend came to the rescue and offered him a room in his basement until he could get back on track. Surely, this would be the final scare—the one that would invoke action. But it wasn't.

All the steps forward in the last couple of years were swiftly erased. He became more distant than ever. Stress and worry never left me. But I suffered silently. I told no one. None of my friends, with their perfect lives, could possibly understand. I feared judgment—that we'd be viewed as "less" because of this silent monster.

When I finally broke and shared our family secret, support and recommendations for rehabilitation facilities poured in unexpectedly. It humbled me, and I realized I was not alone. I began calling the various facilities recommended by my friends. The counsellors on the other end listened with empathy to my desperate pleas, but they told me what I already knew. This was a call only Tyler could make. He needed to be ready to get help, and he just was not there yet.

The months went by, and every ounce of my emotional energy was spent worrying. I gave Tyler the number he needed to call. It sounds so simple—pick up the phone and dial the number. He'd say he was going to call, but the part of him that wanted to change was buried too deep beneath his addiction. Drugs had completely consumed him. He wasn't the son I knew. I learned to live moment by moment, not so different from how I later learned to survive grief.

The call I was praying for was not the one I got. Instead, I was notified that Tyler had been taken to the hospital for a suspected overdose. This was his bottom—the scare he needed. In the days that followed, he found the strength to dial the number. His admission date was set for December 27th. With a date set for Tyler to enter rehab, I allowed myself hope—something I hadn't had for a long time.

We'd always promised Tyler that when he was ready to fight his addiction, we'd be there every step of the way. Up until this day, he was welcome in our home for a visit, but he could not stay for an extended period of time. That was our boundary. Now that he had reached out for help, the boundaries were different. He could stay at our home until his admission date, but we had conditions. He needed to attend Narcotics Anonymous (NA) meetings and be responsible for daily chores around the house. We would be searching his possessions daily, and if drugs were found, he'd be asked to leave immediately. I needed to know that he was clear on the rules and would abide by them. "Yes, I need help," was his reply. The minute I heard those words, I was in my car, making the three-hour trip to pick him up. As we drove home, he opened up to me. He shared everything—the darkness and the secrets—he'd been hiding. It all came out without any filters. I thought I knew, but I had no idea what his life had become. All I could do was listen, with my heart wide open. Then, I reached over and gave his hand a squeeze. "You can beat this," I told him. And I truly believed that he would.

December 27th was only a month away, but it felt like an eternity. Each day, I wondered if I'd find him gone, running back to the lifestyle that still had a pull on him. But he did not run. He stayed and stuck to his obligations. These were hard days for Tyler. I tried my best to understand what he was going through, but I really didn't have a clue.

Slowly, each day got a little better. While we waited for admission day to approach, our relationship improved. We attended NA meetings together and spent many hours just talking. We understood each other in ways we never had before.

While Tyler and Cassie had parted as friends, their love never faded. Despite being separated by thousands of miles, they rekindled their relationship. Cassie wanted to support Tyler on the day he entered the program, so she flew back to Alberta on Christmas Day. Tyler and I picked her up from the airport, excited for the reunion. The bond between us had remained strong, and it felt like she'd never left.

I'll always cherish that Christmas. The boys and I baked cookies together. When they were growing up, making cookies was part of our annual tradition, but as they got older, the roles changed—I baked, and they consumed. It was great to experience the joy of being in the kitchen together as adults. We played games—*Farkle* was that year's choice. Tyler, being the risk taker that he was, usually lost. We had fun teasing him about it. I bought a puzzle for us to work on together, but none of us did very well. Occasionally, someone would find a piece that fit, but we agreed that puzzles weren't our thing. We ate our favourite holiday foods—surprise spread with nachos, shrimp with cocktail sauce, and of course, chocolate snowballs to top it off. That evening, we watched a movie, each of us dozing off at various points. Tyler was the first man down, and once again, we poked some fun at him. It was a good day.

Then, admission day came. I was so afraid to be hopeful. If ever there was a time to pray, this was it. Please God, let this be the turning point. I prayed that this facility would be clean and safe. I prayed that he'd be surrounded by good people. I prayed that he'd stay—that he wouldn't bolt after a few days or maybe even a few hours. I prayed that they could help him. I prayed.

The facility was located in Calgary, about three hours south. Our drive was quiet. Each of us—Tyler, Cassie, and me—lost in our thoughts. It was a frosty winter day, but the sun was shining brightly. On a whim, I pulled off the highway. We stood by the road, enjoying the crispness in the air and the moment together. I pulled out my phone and said, "Let me take a picture of you two." Tyler leaned over and kissed Cassie gently on the forehead, the way he did so often. Little did I know, this would be the last picture I'd have of Tyler and Cassie.

We arrived at our appointed time: 1:00 p.m. As we pulled into the parking lot, I thought, ok, it looks ok. We walked in and somehow it felt exactly right. Our nerves calmed down. Tyler watched the guys milling about and said, "They seem pretty happy here." I smiled and said, "Yeah, they do." I hoped he would be too.

We completed the required paperwork and handed it back to the man at the front desk. Next step: the drug test. Tyler promised that he'd stuck to his commitment, and before long, we were given the "ok." It was time to say our goodbyes. We hugged each other tightly. Cassie and I cried as we turned to leave. In that moment, I could not have been prouder of the strength and courage I saw in my son. Only someone who has walked this road could understand.

The next day, my phone rang. I was eager to hear from him— eager but fearful. Fearful that he'd ask me to come get him— fearful that he'd tell me all the things he hated about being there and how this was going to be a waste of time. When I asked him how he was doing, he replied, "Good" in a rather upbeat tone. "How's your room?" He told me the beds were hard, and with four guys in a room, he didn't sleep very well. But then he followed with, "But it's ok. I think I'll like it here." After hearing those words, my heart filled with relief.

Not only did Tyler stay with the program, he embraced it. He'd tell me about the friends he was making, about the group sessions, and about the activities. He especially loved the weekly group hikes in the nearby Rocky Mountains.

Two weeks into the program, Jeff and I decided it was "safe" to visit him. He had settled in, and the risk of him cornering us with the plea to take him back home seemed minimal. We walked through the front door, and there was my Tyler strutting down the hallway with a smile and a swagger that I'd forgotten existed. He gave us one of his famous hugs and showed us to the café area where we'd sat just two weeks earlier. Only this time, there was no angst, only elation. As we talked, I looked at him in awe. It was like I was seeing him, the real Tyler, for the first time in a very long time. He was clear-headed, calm, and content. He was happy.

My heart swelled. I looked to the heavens and whispered a silent "thank you." I felt lighter than I had for years. I envisioned him inspiring others with his story. Perhaps he would take on a volunteer role, helping other youths struggling with addiction. I wondered what great things life had in store for him, what kind of job he'd get, where he'd settle down, and the family he might have one day. It felt good to think about the future.

Seven weeks later, he graduated from the program. Jeff and I were excited to share this day with Tyler, and we arrived with plenty of time to spare. Tyler met us in the dining hall, with hugs of course. He pulled up a chair between us and asked if we wanted to see his notebook. It was filled with art and poetry—each page a creative expression of his emotional journey. I read his poems and cried. Such vulnerability he'd put into words.

Graduation day at the facility was very different from the ceremonies familiar to most of us. Instead of hundreds of graduates, often there were only one or two. Instead of family members clamouring for a seat, many graduates had no one to applaud them. Their parents did not take them shopping for a fancy new suit. Instead, they wore the clothes they came with, or perhaps they found something a little dressier in the donation area. The goal for the future was the same for everyone: to stay clean.

When someone enters the program, they are given a black rock. At the end of the program, they exchange the black rock for a white one that has been picked out especially for them. The program director described why one particular rock was picked for Tyler. He said it was a shiny rock, symbolizing all the potential he saw in Tyler. But the rock also had a few blemishes, signifying the work ahead. It was a perfect analogy for Tyler's journey. Next, his case manager spoke. He shared how Tyler had become a leader among his peers, of the respect he had earned both from staff and residents, and of the opportunities in his future. Then, it was Tyler's turn. Picking exactly the right words was important to Tyler. He told me, "I want my speech to be emotional and hopefully bring a few tears to the crowd." Nervously, he approached the front of the room.

I guess it all started from a pain deep down within that I never acknowledged. Something I had bottled inside and carried around with me. Never sure of how to be a real man, I found pleasure in other things: drugs. They took that pain away and made me believe I was something I was not. Having two dads walk out of my life—one at age five, the next when I was 14—smoking weed seemed to be the best way to deal with my emotions. I was just too scared and not ready to feel. Keeping that inside me seemed to cause my life to be in turmoil. I thought it was unfair when my real dad was diagnosed with MS and dementia. We never had the kind of relationship I wanted, and now there seemed to be no way we ever would. I started smoking weed just to get shit off my mind. Never dealing with my problems, I seemed to blame everyone else, and it started to ruin me. When my mom remarried, I couldn't imagine dealing with that again, so I got a job on a service rig up north and moved out. That was a huge mistake, as I was introduced to all kinds of drugs that I seemed to love. They buried my pain deep. Never thinking one day I would have to face those demons. Creating a distance with my mom that grew with every day, month, year seemed to be the best way to hide the person I was, never realizing what it was doing to her. I started to think maybe it's not everyone else—maybe it's me. But that didn't stop me. I was too far gone in my addiction to know any better. Using cocaine and opiates daily just seemed to be the only way. This went on for three years. I started to slack off, miss work, stopped paying my bills. Everything was falling apart, but I couldn't stop. Eventually, I lost my job but just continued on selling to fuel my addiction and felt everything was fine—I was too far gone. All that mattered was getting high. Then, as everything does, it came to an end. Never knowing how I had gotten so far down, despite being raised in a good home, learning good ethics and good morals, coming from a straight-cut family, I was definitely the black sheep. When I woke up in the hospital not knowing what had happened, I knew I needed change, needed help. Calling my mom and telling her the wretched, horrible person I had become was the hardest thing I ever had to do. She immediately came and picked me up. Looking for the best program we could find, reaching out to people—it changed my life. I want to say thanks to everyone in this room for helping me through this. Thanks to my awesome instructors for their understanding. All the people I've met here, it's closer than friendship—it's like a brotherhood to me. It's better than any friend I've made over the past 10 years. I want to say thanks to my excellent counsellor Jacob for helping me through all the hard parts and teaching me how to have fun sober. None of this would have been possible without all of you but, most of all, my perfect mom for bringing me home and never closing that door. You saved my life, and I promise to never put you through that pain again.

TYLER

6

NO SAFE PLACE

After graduating from the program, Tyler decided to stay in transitional housing. He'd be in the same building but on a different floor—a move that might seem inconsequential, but to Tyler it held great significance. This move symbolized progression. He would have more freedom in his schedule, but still have access to his counsellor, NA meetings, and a peer group who understood addiction. Most importantly, the "no drugs" rule would continue to be enforced. He'd be safe there.

The move to transitional housing was not his initial intention. He wanted to jump back into his old life, convinced he could stay clean.

Despite all I'd learned about addiction, I was still so naive. I thought that completing the program meant it was all uphill from there—that the toughest part was over. Little did I know, this was just the beginning.

I'd continued to seek counselling on my own while Tyler was in the program. I wanted to be the best support to Tyler that I could and that meant understanding addiction better, a world still so foreign to me. I learned that often my best intentions were impeding his recovery and my counsellor helped to keep me on the right path. I was excited to tell him about Tyler's graduation day and his plans to stay in transitional housing. I thought he would congratulate me and tell me our journey had been completed. But instead, he shattered my euphoria. He told me there was a very high probability that Tyler would relapse. "Why would that be?" I asked him, stunned by what I was hearing. I told him about Tyler's speech and of how he promised to never put me through that again. How could he say these things one minute and relapse the next? It made no sense. My counsellor reminded me that addiction does not follow the rules and defies all logic. In the life of an addict, seven weeks clean is only a blink.

After graduation, Tyler relapsed just as I had been warned. It was difficult for me to understand the power of addiction, but the counselling had helped me prepare. The advice? Don't get angry but confront the situation. Be clear this is not ok but in a way that makes him feel supported. It was an emotional balancing act. I wasn't perfect at it, but I had come a long way. I didn't bury my head or allow Tyler to deny what I knew was true. As a consequence of his relapse, Tyler was evicted from his housing facility for five days. Should I let him spend it on the street or bring him to our home? Leaning on the advice of the experts, we brought Tyler home. Tyler knew this wasn't a given—that the consequence could have been much different—and he was grateful for our support. We faced the challenge head on and talked together in ways we never had before. The conversation was open and honest and without excuses. When I asked him why, his answer was, "I felt like I earned it. That I could enjoy it one last time and then get back on track." I was firm that next time we would not rescue him. Tyler saw a new-found strength in me and did not question this. Jeff did not allow anger to get in his way. Instead, he listened calmly, intent on understanding. Together, we worked through the ebbs and flows. Challenges that once divided us now made us stronger.

After the required five days were up, Tyler was ready and excited to return to his room in transitional housing. Despite the ups and downs, he continued on his path to recovery. Over time, he got a job doing apartment building repairs and renovations. He was learning new skills and working alongside his best friend. Tyler was happy. Jeff and I were solid. No discord. Everything exactly as it should be.

Two months later, the police arrived at my workplace to tell me Tyler had died. In the place where I encouraged him to stay—the place where I thought he'd be the safest—he died. Just when I thought worry was behind me, he died. When his future finally seemed bright, he died. With help right outside his door and with support, counsellors, and roommates just steps away, still he died. I did everything to try and protect him, but still he slipped away, quietly, peacefully, in the safety of his bed.

Many people expected me to lash out in anger at the facility where he stayed. I'm sure many people would have. I sent him there to get help—to be safe. It was a drug-free facility! But as much as I couldn't protect him, neither could they. No one could.

I wasn't angry at them. I knew they carried far more guilt than any human should. They were good people, and I had the utmost respect for the work that they did. Tyler admired everyone there. So did I.

Instead, the universe bore the brunt of my anger. This wasn't supposed to be the ending—it was supposed to be a new beginning. WHY NOW? He wanted to marry and have children. He loved kids. Why didn't I get the chance to see him become a dad? And what about Jordan—he didn't deserve to lose his only brother. Why was the universe punishing us?

Sometimes I would yell to the heavens, "WHY?!!" It was as if Tyler himself was sending the message clearly back to me, "It was time for me to go." And I'd reply, "I know you had to go. But why? I miss you so much." As much as I hated how his story ended, I knew that this was meant to be his journey.

It took time for my anger to subside. When it did, I could see things differently. Instead of focusing on what I'd lost, I began to see all that I'd been given. He could have been taken even sooner. Every day I had with him was a gift. I got to see the "real" Tyler. The one I always knew was there. I got to see him excited about life. I understood him better than ever before. Our love was strong. Memories of our last days together, every conversation, every hug, every "I love you"—I would forever cherish these gifts.

7

DIMES AND OTHER SIGNS

The notion of an afterlife has always intrigued me. I'd read the John Edward book, *Crossing Over*, and its stories seemed plausible. But it was more of a cognitive reaction than a belief that resonated in my soul. *Before,* whether or not a person's spirit or energy continued to exist after the death of their physical body honestly didn't matter that much to me. I thought I'd find out when my time came. John Edward's stories of connections to those who had crossed over opened my mind to the possibility, but the stories were just that . . . stories. I couldn't relate to the feelings that accompanied these stories. *After,* that changed.

It was like I'd joined a secret club with membership exclusive to those who believed in spirits. It was hard to know who was "in" because you dared not speak freely of this for fear of judgment. People I'd known for many years suspected I might have joined the club since losing someone you loved deeply was usually the catalyst. Friends who hadn't previously shared their beliefs, now delicately tested the waters. Once they knew that I also believed in spirits, the stories flowed freely.

One person asked me if I'd thought about seeing a medium. New to the club, I thought that I'd have to travel great distances and pay extravagant fees for a reading with a real medium. Then, someone from the club told me of a medium who comes to Camrose a few times each year. She'd seen her previously and found her to be very good. Dumbfounded, I googled her, and sure enough, there she was—a self-proclaimed medium. It all seemed so normal . . . "to book an appointment, click here." I clicked.

I was anxious in the days leading up to my appointment. My heart yearned to receive one last message from Tyler, but what if she couldn't connect with him? What would that mean? That I was silly to think his energy was around me, showing me signs? That dead was dead and nothing more? As much as I feared no connection, my greater fear was that he'd be regretful and that he'd beg for a do-over so he could be back on earth with us. Knowing I was powerless to comfort him caused me great angst. I needed to know he was at peace.

Finally, the day arrived. I tried to be nonchalant but hope burned bright.

The medium introduced herself and complimented me on the colour of my shirt. I smiled and thanked her, thinking this was a rather ordinary comment for someone who talks to spirits. I followed her to the backroom where she conducted her readings. She sat on one side of a small table—I on the other. She offered me a pen and paper so I could take notes, but I was too nervous. She became quiet as if listening to something only she could hear. The skeptic in me thought, good act. But the believer in me was curious. She asked, "Who wakes you up in the middle of the night?" It could have been a fishing expedition or a lucky guess, but it struck me as profound. Ever since Tyler's passing, I'd felt compelled to get out of bed around 3:00 a.m. It was an abrupt awakening, like something urging me to leave the bedroom. I'd sit alone in the stillness of the night and just "feel" him with me. There was a peacefulness about it. Tears welled up in my eyes, and my stomach flip-flopped. I replied, "It's my son, Tyler." Then she said, "Yes . . . Ty." It's a pretty easy guess that his nickname was "Ty," but still it felt good to hear her say this.

She described him. "He's handsome." True, but what mother doesn't think that? "He's funny," she said with a laugh. Yup, right again, but it was a 50/50 chance of getting that right. "He thought he was invincible. Here for a good time, not a long time . . . does that sound like your Tyler?" "It sure does," I replied. "He likes to be the life of the party." Bang on again. "He didn't intend to die, but he played a role in his passing. Would that be correct?" "Yes, that's right," I replied. "He wants you to know that he understands everything you did, you did out of love. That you were trying to help him."

I listened in awe as the messages continued to come. She went on to tell me that he liked the party his friends had for him. After the funeral service, Tyler's friends gathered out at his stepbrother's acreage. They had a bonfire and sat around singing while Michael played guitar. It was exactly the kind of evening Tyler would have loved.

Then she said, "So you've found his dimes." I nodded, reaching for the Kleenex I'd noticed earlier. "You'll find more." (And we did.)

She continued, "You feel like a bird is following you." It sounds crazy, but that's exactly how I felt. Everywhere I went, I heard this bird singing, like he was singing right to me. When I went for walks, he sang to me all along the way. Every time I sat in our backyard, I heard my bird. One time I even heard him while sitting in my car waiting for a red light at a busy intersection. He was **always** there. I wanted to ask someone, "What's with the birds this year?" because I thought surely everyone must notice. But another part of me decided it was best to keep quiet. I'd never experienced anything like it. To hear her acknowledge it left me feeling stunned.

On she went. "Tyler says Happy Mother's Day." I thought it was lame for her to say this. Too ordinary. Too predictable. "He tried to call," she said. The reading went from lame to pathetic. Pretty sure there's no cell service in heaven, I thought. What a crazy comment for her to make. "Don't worry, he'll try again." Whatever, I thought. Parts of the reading were absolutely divine, while others left me deflated. I decided to take comfort in the parts that brought me peace and let go of the rest.

That night, as I was lying in bed reading, my cell phone pinged. It was a text from an unknown contact. "Hi, it's Tyson." My son, Ty . . . Tyson . . . now that's some crazy shit, I thought. If the text had read, "Hi, it's Tyler," well that would've been downright creepy. I sat frozen, staring at my phone and looking for an explanation that made sense. I never gave the medium my cell phone number, so it wasn't her playing mind games. I never told anyone the details of this session. I don't know anyone named Tyson. And who sends a text message that says, "Hi, it's me" and nothing more? Feeling bewildered, I decided to reply back, "Sorry but I don't know who this is." His reply, "Sorry wrong num." That's exactly how Tyler would've answered—never using full words. I smiled. Maybe there's cell phone service in heaven after all.

My dime-finding experiences started about a month after Tyler's passing. I was on leave from work and filled my days with therapy. This therapy took many different forms. There was the traditional therapy, like my weekly one-hour sessions with a psychologist and the Tuesday evening group therapy sessions. Then, there was the therapy that was just for my soul—the things that brought a sense of peace to me. Reading, exercise, and spending quiet time in nature had always been activities I enjoyed, but now I craved them.

As part of my therapy, I asked Jeff to build me a garden—a quiet place where I could connect with the earth. I loved my "play time" in the dirt, watching new life grow. It was a place where I felt connected to Tyler. One morning, as I was enjoying my meditation in the dirt, something shiny caught my eye. A single dime lying on the cement patio next to my garden. It was so out of place—this dime lying in our backyard where only I had been. I stood and stared at it. My mind was searching for a logical explanation, afraid to let my heart believe it was a sign from heaven. I picked it up and clasped it tightly to my heart. Then, I looked skyward and whispered, "I love you, Ty."

My next dime appeared on my first day back to work. In many ways, I was ready to return to work. But another part of me dreaded walking into the place where I had learned of Tyler's passing, afraid of being transported back to that horrible day. It was a nice morning, so I walked to work. I thought it might help ground me and prepare me for this day. Just blocks before I arrived at the office, smack dab in front of me on the sidewalk, was one dime. I picked up my dime and smiled. I knew Tyler's spirit was telling me, "You'll be ok, Mom."

Over the months ahead, I continued to find the occasional dime, always a single dime, often at a significant time or place. I told Jeff my dime stories, and he did what good husbands do— he listened and smiled politely. It wasn't that he didn't believe. He just couldn't relate. He was happy I was finding comfort in these findings, but he held a healthy amount of skepticism. I'm glad he did because it helped me keep things in perspective. Still, I wished that Jeff and I could share this experience together. Later that summer, I got my wish.

Jeff was outside doing some yard work, and I was inside doing chores. He called to me in an uncharacteristically abrupt tone, "Come here." "What's wrong?" I asked as I ran towards the door. I was worried that he'd hurt himself. When I reached the door, he pointed to the bottom step where one single dime was lying. "Did you put this here?" he asked. "No, it wasn't me," I replied. Rather befuddled, he continued, "Well, how did it get here?" I looked at him and smiled. He paused, waiting for me to explain, but I couldn't. Now, he understood.

In the years to follow, Jeff and I would continue to find the occasional dime. We'd share in the excitement, wondering what message Tyler was sending us. Jeff no longer worried that I'd bought a one-way ticket on the crazy train, and I was grateful that, together, we shared a spiritual connection with Tyler.

I'm not the only one with dime stories. Cassie has a few too, but this is the first and my favourite.

While living apart, Tyler and Cassie talked on the phone almost every night before bed. During their last conversation and before Tyler drifted away forever, Cassie told him she had joined a slow-pitch team. She told him that she was nervous, but

Tyler reassured her. "You'll do great," he said. Athletics came easy to both of them. Then, she told him she'd try to get his favourite jersey number: lucky #13.

When Cassie returned to her life back home following Tyler's passing, she was given jersey #13, just as she had hoped. She wore it proudly. It was only fitting that she'd find her first dime at a ball tournament. She was in the public washroom facilities between games. As she entered the bathroom stall, she saw three dimes on the floor, waiting just for her. We joked that he lacked in the romance department! Cassie knew that Tyler was proudly cheering her on.

One of Tyler's closest friends, and Cassie's best friend, was Erica. The three of them shared a deep bond and were inseparable. Erica was an unexpected comfort to me in the years to follow. Although she had a close friendship with Tyler, I'd only met her once. Our connection was created through our mutual love for Tyler. I received many notes from her, but this is one of my favourites.

For some reason, out of the blue, I wanted to go to the library. I haven't gone in years, and to be honest, I haven't really had an interest. But the day after Tyler's birthday, something was pushing me to go. So I went. As I pulled into the parking lot, I saw a lady with a huge bouquet of red roses with black decor on them. They caught my eye in seconds. They smelled and looked amazing. I couldn't stop looking at them. They reminded me of the flowers from Tyler's Celebration of Life.

Shortly after admiring them, I went into the library still in awe. The lady told me to take a seat. While I was waiting to be signed up for a library card, I noticed a little basket of swans. They were all beat up, misshapen, and different colours, except for one white one. It was sitting on top of the others one, staring at me, I swear! I asked the lady if I could take it, and she said yes. I was so happy! Later, I looked up the meaning of them, and they symbolize peace and love. So crazy!

Wandering around the library, I turned into an aisle and noticed a book lying on the floor. I picked it up and saw that is was a wolf book! Tyler, Cassie, and I always used to joke that we were lone wolves until we found each other. Then, we became a pack! Cassie and I even bought him a little wolf sculpture that he looooved. It's all such little things, but when I look at the big picture, they are huge things! And he was reaching out. ♥ ♥ ♥

When I think of Tyler in the physical form, my heart aches to hear his voice, to see him smile, and to hug him harder than ever before. I'd give anything for one last time with him. While it breaks my heart to know I'll never get this chance, in another way, I've never felt closer to him. I'm learning how to have a spiritual relationship with my son. I can't see him, hear him, or touch him, but I know that his beautiful energy surrounds me always. I've learned to think of Tyler, not as I once knew him, but as he is now—my beautiful white light.

8

PERFECT STRANGERS

I n the months and years following Tyler's passing, healing came slowly and in ways I never anticipated. Family, close friends, Mother Nature, and time—they all played a role. But the most profound was the unexpected kindness of random (or not-so-random) strangers. *Before,* I would have viewed these encounters as sheer coincidence. *After,* I believe these strangers were put in my path and that our lives were meant to intersect. Brief as these encounters were, they filled my cup and left me with memories that will always be with me.

To all my perfect strangers, thank you. You shone a light when I needed it most.

A few days following Tyler's service, I decided to donate some of the flowers we'd received. They were magnificent and brought me much peace. I wanted to share their beauty with someone else—someone who might also need comforting. The Camrose hospital is where I decided they should go. I'm not sure why the hospital. It was a place that held no significance, yet it felt right.

I picked the bouquets that I wanted to share. Jeff drove while I held them steady. Knowing how fragile I was, Jeff offered to take them inside. But it was important that I be the one to deliver them. I gathered my bouquets, one in each arm, and walked through the sliding doors towards the front desk. The receptionist greeted me with a warm smile. "How can I help you?" she asked. I told her I had some flowers to donate. "Is there any particular unit you want them to go to?" I started to cry. I'd thought I could get through this one simple act without tears. I told her the flowers were from my son's funeral. Her face softened, and she looked at me with empathy. Tenderly she said, "I lost a daughter."

I had felt so alone in my grieving. Despite much support, I was certain no one could possibly understand what I was going through. Until now. She told me about her daughter, and I told her about my son. Then she said, "I know you can't imagine it now, but you will be ok." From anyone else, these words would have been meaningless. But from her, they gave me hope.

Our conversation lasted only minutes. I didn't learn her name, and I'll likely never meet her again. But hearing her say, "You will survive this" made me walk out of that hospital a little stronger than when I walked in.

Every young adult who moves away from home has possessions they no longer use but aren't ready to part with. These possessions land in a box, stored away in a closet. One of Tyler's "not needed but not ready to let go of" items were his rollerblades. They sat in our basement closet for years. When it was time for my annual purge, I'd often put them into the donation box. But just before delivering my box of donations, I'd invariably change my mind and back in the closet they'd go. Four days before Tyler's passing, I decided it was finally time to let them go, so I posted his rollerblades on a local Buy and Sell website. Within a few hours, a lady messaged me, "I'll take them." No questions asked. We made arrangements for her to pick them up the following night. The next day, I received a text from her. Something had come up, and she couldn't make it. "No problem," I replied. "Just let me know when it works better."

The week after Tyler's passing, she messaged me, asking if she could come and pick up the rollerblades. How life changes. The week before, I was decluttering closets. This week, I was mourning the death of my son. A week ago, I felt good about a little extra room in my closet. Now, I couldn't bear to part with them. I wrote back, "Susan, something terrible has happened to our family. This past week we lost our son, Tyler. The rollerblades belonged to him. It feels right that you should have them, but I'm not ready to part with them yet. I'll let you know when the time is right." She replied with her heartfelt condolences.

Later that evening, Susan arrived at our door. I'd never met her before, so I didn't make the connection. In her hands, she held a big pot of homemade butternut squash soup and biscuits. I was so moved by this act of kindness—that a complete stranger had taken the time to prepare this wonderful meal for us. But it was more than that. My weekly shopping list consists of the usual:

eggs, milk, bread, fresh fruit . . . but for me, butternut squash soup is also a staple. Happy Planet's Berkeley Butternut Squash Soup is my favourite quick lunch during the workweek. How could she have possibly known this was my favourite soup? Coincidence, maybe . . . but I believe Tyler sent her to me. He was comforting me in the only way he could—by sending me an angel.

In the weeks to follow, I thought about the string of events leading up to the day I met Susan. What kept me from getting rid of his rollerblades in years past? And what happened that prevented Susan from picking up his rollerblades on the date we'd initially set? And why butternut squash soup? Wouldn't something more traditional, like chicken noodle, be a better choice for someone you'd never met?

Several weeks later, I sent a note to Susan, thanking her for her kindness. I told her I was ready to part with Tyler's rollerblades and knew, without a doubt, I'd found the perfect home for them. We made arrangements—I'd drop them off at her house that evening. When I arrived, she greeted me with a warm hug and introduced me to her husband. They felt like long-lost friends, not strangers I'd only just met. Then, her husband asked if we could say a prayer for Tyler. "That would be beautiful," I replied. And there, in the home of these strangers, the three of us stood in a circle holding hands, tears rolling down my cheek as I listened to this man's prayer for my son.

Before I left, I asked Susan if she'd share her soup recipe with me. "It was absolutely delicious," I told her. She paused for a moment, thinking. Then she said, "I can't remember where I found that recipe. Give me a minute, and I'll see if I can find it." A few minutes later, she came back from her kitchen and said, "I'm sorry. I found it online, but I'm not sure where." Until then,

I assumed it was one of her favourites and that's why she made it for me. Now, I know there was something greater at work. I'll never forget Susan and her fabulous butternut squash soup.

One of my favourite places in Camrose is the walking trail around Mirror Lake, which is a small man-made lake in the middle of the city. I've spent many hours there. One day, I saw something that I'd never seen before. Someone had written inspiring messages with sidewalk chalk all along the path—messages, such as "Take time to smell the flowers," "You are loved," "Have you thanked someone today?" and my favourite, "Even in darkness, there is a glimmer of hope." It felt like they were written just for me.

I'll never know who wrote them, and that person will never know how deeply their words touched my soul. Thank you, my perfect stranger, for sending such powerful messages out into the universe.

Every fall, Jeff and I take a camping vacation. Usually, we plan our next vacation as soon as the previous one ends. 2015 was no different. But when we planned this trip, I never imagined we'd be taking it while grieving.

We thought about cancelling. I felt empty inside and knew it wouldn't hold the excitement we'd originally anticipated. Our plan was to drive along the Oregon coast. I thought the beauty and tranquility might be healing, so we decided to go.

At the midpoint of our travels, we pulled into a "first-come, first-served" campground near Florence. Travelling in the off-season, we were confident we'd find a vacant site. We drove through the campground loop a few times, scouting out our options and finally deciding on the site we liked best.

After setting up camp, we decided to take a walk along the nearby beach. The crashing waves were mesmerizing, and with hardly anyone in sight, we could be alone with our thoughts. It was exactly what we needed.

Returning to our campground, we saw we had neighbours on each side of us. Later we discovered they were travelling together and had been coming to this particular campground for years. The site we'd chosen was one of their favourites, so they decided to take the sites on each side of us instead. They would walk past our site several times a day, and we'd give a smile or friendly wave.

One evening, we happened to be near the campground road as our neighbour, Jack, was walking by with his poodle. He stopped to say hello. Jack had an ease about him, and his presence felt comfortable. Our conversation started in the usual way it does with a stranger . . . "Where are you from? Have you been here before? What did you do today?" How the conversation went from small talk to something far deeper, I'm not entirely sure. He shared that he was grieving the loss of his wife, his partner for the last 50 years. He shared that his friends were the best, but they did not understand. They still had each other. We told him we understood—we were grieving as well. It was a powerful moment. Each of us grieving, now brought together. We shared tears, and then he hugged me. The warmth went through to my soul—it reminded me of Tyler's hugs.

While this trip was healing, nothing brought me more joy than this random encounter. I'll never forget Jack, his grey poodle, and his powerful hug.

———————

Mason met his perfect stranger in an airport. It was a few months *after*, and he was on his way to Hawaii with a friend. Both had gone through tough life situations recently and decided this trip would be good for them. We hadn't communicated much since Tyler's service, just the occasional check in. Then, I received this text from him:

Hey, yesterday I was in the Vancouver airport lounge waiting for our connecting flight, saw some random dude, and just started talking. Turns out he was one of Tyler's friends. He had not heard. We had hugs and tears. What a surreal experience. Some dude just sitting alone in a huge airport, and we connect. I did not know him, and he did not recognize me. This was not chance; I cannot describe how perfect this turned out. I thought I was taking this trip to help someone else out—turns out that our boy is helping me.

———————

I can't write about perfect strangers without writing about Debbie. Debbie is Erica's mom. I met her on a cold, wintery day during one of my trips to see Tyler. As I pulled up to Tyler's place, she was heading out of her house a few doors down. She waved at me from her driveway. "You must be Tyler's mom," she hollered. "I'm Debbie, Erica's mom. How were the roads?" "Terrible," I shouted back. She was on her way to work, and it was cold, so the conversation was quick. I never thought about Debbie again . . . until *after*.

Debbie became my saviour. She sent me notes at all the right times, always finding the perfect words. She continued this long after most people stopped. She understood how difficult special occasions were. On my birthday, she wrote a heartfelt note, acknowledging how difficult this day must be. She had flowers delivered to our home on Christmas. With every word and every act of kindness, Debbie gave me strength.

She didn't need to reach out to me. We weren't friends. We were barely acquaintances. But she did. She had empathy and found exactly the words I needed to hear. *Before,* she was just a person I had one brief conversation with. *After,* I felt blessed to have her in my life.

Tucker is our dog. According to the DNA test, his dad was a German shepherd/border collie/Great Pyrenees, and his mom was a German shepherd/collie/St. Bernard cross. Whatever he is, he couldn't be more lovable. Here's the story of how Tucker came to be ours.

Some people are dog people, and some aren't. Up until the day Tucker came to us, I was not a dog person. I didn't dislike dogs and found them cute enough, but I had no desire to own one. Tyler, however, loved dogs. He always wanted a pet growing up, but that wasn't in the cards. Taking care of two boys was enough, never mind adding a dog to the mix. "You can have a dog when you're grown up, living on your own," I'd tell him. And that's exactly what he did. Tyler adopted a dog from a local shelter.

I wasn't happy when I found out—it wasn't the right time for Tyler to take on pet ownership. And why such a big dog? But it was out of my hands … Tyler had a dog. I never formed an attachment to the dog because first, I wasn't a dog person, and second, I didn't agree with Tyler having a dog.

After, Tucker stayed with Gerry, one of Tyler's friends. I was happy with this arrangement, and I knew he'd be well taken care of. That winter, Gerry decided to move back to eastern Canada and needed to find a new home for Tucker. I told Jeff, "We can't let Tucker go back to the shelter. Tyler rescued him. We have to find him a good home." We put out the word, asking if anyone would like a dog. This might have been easier if Tucker was a little lapdog, but he weighed 85 pounds. I was relieved when a co-worker of Jeff's agreed to take him, knowing we'd found a good home. We made arrangements to pick Tucker up and take him to his new owner.

Jeff and I were nervous about picking up Tucker. Neither of us had any experience with dogs and didn't know what to expect. We covered the back seat of our truck with an old blanket, packed some water and a bowl, and headed off. We had arranged a halfway meeting point with Gerry. We pulled in, spotted his truck, and parked beside him. We talked for a bit. He told us Tucker had travelled well, but he was a bit anxious. Then, he let Tucker out of his vehicle. We wondered if he'd be scared to come with us, but it was quite the opposite—he ran to us like we were long-lost friends. He snuggled up to Jeff first and then to me. He jumped into the back seat of our truck like it was "his truck." While Jeff drove, I petted Tucker and talked to him in a soft cooing voice. My heart was melting—an emotion I never anticipated. I could tell Jeff felt it too. There was an instant bond, and already we loved him.

Our plan was to keep Tucker for one night before handing him over to his new owner. I was happy to have this extra day with Tucker. "Do you think we should keep him?" I asked Jeff. "It doesn't make sense," was Jeff's logical reply. And he was right. We were both away at work all day, our yard wasn't fenced, and we knew nothing about dogs. There were many logical reasons why we shouldn't keep him, but yet, it felt like Tucker was meant to be with us.

Despite the pull on our heartstrings, we continued with our plan, and Jeff took Tucker to his new home the next morning. I cried. Yes, this non-dog person cried over a dog I'd known only 24 hours. "It's for the best," Jeff reminded me. And with that, Jeff took Tucker to his new home.

The next day, Jeff asked Tucker's new owner how it was going. "Well, not so great," he replied. He felt bad because he knew it was important for us to find Tucker a good home. "He's not settling in and doesn't seem to be getting along with my other dog." Without hesitation, Jeff said, "I'll come and get him." We didn't need to have a conversation about it; we both knew Tucker belonged with us. Nothing could have made me happier.

Tucker has brought us more love and comfort than we ever imagined. He's part of our family. And yes, I am now a full-fledged dog person. Sometimes, I wonder if Tyler rescued Tucker for us. Of all my perfect strangers, no one is more perfect than our Tucker!

9

WHAT I'VE LEARNED

've learned many things on this journey. In many ways, I'm a better person because of it. While I wish there had been an easier way to arrive at this place, this was the path intended for me.

It was easy to focus on what I'd lost. I'd never see Tyler marry or become a dad. I'd never hear his voice or his laugh again. His face would only exist in my memory. But in time, I learned to be grateful for what I had. Of course, I will always miss him, but I had Tyler for 25 years—that makes for a lot of great memories. I was the first person to hold him, my baby boy. I got to be his mom. Of all the moms in the world, he picked me—how great is that! I rocked him to sleep, saw his first steps, and heard his first words. I cried on his first day of school. Jordan grew up with an amazing brother. I cheered for him at hockey games and soccer games—always proud of my #13. My heart fluttered when he told me about his first love and hurt for his first breakup. I watched him grow from a boy to a man. We shared countless hugs and enough "I love yous" to last a lifetime. Now, when my mind wanders to all that could have been, I take a deep breath. Then, I give thanks for all that was.

I learned to let go of negative emotions. Anger, bitterness, self-pity, guilt—they needed to be with me for a while. How could they not? I needed to spend time with each of them and let them work their way through. In a way, I became attached to them and letting go was hard. But the weight was too heavy. I had to release them.

I'm humbler and less judgmental—something I learned from Tyler. I always thought I was the one teaching him, but it turns out that he left me with some pretty powerful lessons. Perhaps his own struggles made him feel deeply for others, or maybe it was just innate. As his life became more difficult, his compassion only grew stronger.

I've learned the power of simple acts of kindness. It's easy to get busy, to think it doesn't matter, or that someone else will step up. But it DOES matter. In fact, nothing matters more. Small gestures, a kind word, a smile—they can change someone's day. *Before*, I'd worry too much about getting it exactly right—finding the perfect words or performing a grandiose act. *After*, I realized getting it perfect doesn't matter. Trying, making an effort—that's what matters.

I've given myself permission to be happy and to enjoy life. Initially, moments of pleasure felt wrong, like I was doing a dis-service to Tyler by loving my life when his had been taken. But now, I feel it's my duty, my obligation, to live my best life ever. And in doing so, I will honour my son.

I worry less. My worrying did not save Tyler. I could not have worried more, yet it did not save him. It served no purpose.

Before, decision-making was something to lament over and to stress about. *After*, I learned to be much more patient. The process can't be rushed. The answer will come when the time is right. I've learned to listen to my heart—it knows when the answer has arrived.

I've learned how wonderful it is to simply "be." *Before,* self-worth was measured by accomplishment. *After,* I learned the power of stillness. It's warm and beautiful in this place of quiet solitude.

I understand the importance of "soul therapy"—the activities where time stands still and you completely lose yourself. Time in nature became my sanctuary. A place where I could feel my energy connect with his energy. It was a place of healing. I felt showered by radiant love—perhaps his, perhaps the universe's.

It goes without saying that my journey through grief was heartbreaking and devastating. I worried it might shut down my soul, but I vowed to let my heart be open. I learned to be kind to myself throughout the process, not to run from it, but not to get lost in it either. Tyler is part of me now—as if a little piece of his precious spirit has been sprinkled into my heart. I can feel him . . . it's beautiful and comforting.

Often, I hear people say he was taken too soon—a thought I've had many times too. But I've come to believe that whatever he needed to accomplish on this earth had been completed. He was taken at exactly "his time."

I have an inner peace and acceptance now. I believe we are not as in control of our lives as we like to think. The universe or God or an angel—whatever you call that thing that is so much bigger than all of us—has a plan. We may not understand it or like it. But there is a plan. With every experience, there is a lesson. And with every lesson, we grow. Every hurt, every joy, every obstacle—they all have a purpose.

I'm ok with not knowing where life is leading me or under-standing why. In time, it will become clear. And when it does, it will be exactly as it was meant to be.

ACKNOWLEDGMENTS

Writing this book was one of the most challenging undertakings I've pursued. My deepest thanks and appreciation to the following people who played an important role in my story, both on and off the pages:

Kellie Garrett - This book would not have happened without you. Thank you for telling me I had a story, for guiding me, and for many hours of review and editing advice. You are a beautiful soul.

Michelle Verge at Friesen Press – Thank you for guiding me through the publication process. You were fantastic to work with!

Kathie Toohey, Bonnie Corradetti, Des Rattray, Glen Svenungard, Elsbeth von der Burg, Janita Van de Velde, Kimberley Rideout, Sharon Eistetter – Thank you providing valuable feedback on my manuscript prior to publication. Whether we've shared a life-long bond or a brief connection, you've inspired me. I'm so grateful our life paths intersected.

My husband, Jeff - You are my rock—then, now and always. Thank you for walking by my side. I love you.

My son, Jordan - You make everything in my life shine brighter. Dream big and always listen to your heart.